# Now and Then

Joanna van Kool trained first at the Royal Central School for Drama in London. On graduation, she came to Australia and worked freelance for the ABC Education and Drama Departments in Queensland and taught Drama at both primary and secondary school levels before teaching English, History and Drama for over twenty years at various secondary schools in both Queensland and New South Wales. She gained her Masters in Creative Writing at Sydney University, where she was lucky enough to have the late Dr Noel Rowe as her tutor in poetry. In 2014, she self-published an historical novel, *The Followers*, about three generations of women in her family, and she has recently completed another novel inspired by her environmental concerns. While she has always written in one form or another, she finds that poetry gives her both a challenge and satisfaction in its necessity for the most careful choice of words.

Jo van Kool

# Now and Then

*Now and Then*
ISBN 978 1 76041 984 4
Copyright © Jo van Kool 2020
Cover painting: Brenda Eldridge

First published 2020 by
**GINNINDERRA PRESS**
PO Box 3461 Port Adelaide 5015
www.ginninderrapress.com.au

# Contents

Now
| | |
|---|---|
| Between the Wings | 9 |
| Memories | 10 |
| Maybe | 11 |
| Getting Started | 12 |
| A Lady Bird? | 13 |
| Some Birds and a Cat | 14 |
| The Crested Pigeons at my Window | 16 |
| Suburban street trees | 17 |
| Compositions | 18 |
| Winter rain | 19 |
| Life in a raindrop | 20 |
| A Roseville Garden | 21 |
| Night Life | 22 |
| Drought | 23 |
| The Nameless | 24 |
| In northern winter | 25 |
| Sea Pictures | 26 |
| Sharks | 27 |
| The Innocence of Whales | 28 |
| A visitor to my garden | 29 |
| A Bus Ride | 30 |
| The Artists' Camp at Sirius Cove | 31 |
| Nostalgia | 32 |
| Summer Sunset | 33 |
| Boonah – an Exhibition by Disability Artists | 34 |
| A Breakfast Jam | 35 |
| Letting Go | 36 |
| Destruction | 37 |
| Where once I walked | 38 |

| | |
|---|---|
| A view over the fence | 39 |
| Reality | 40 |
| Remnants | 41 |
| Transgressions | 42 |
| Contrasts | 43 |
| On Flinders Island | 44 |
| Northern Territory Shame | 45 |
| Difference | 46 |
| At this Point in Time | 47 |

## And Then

| | |
|---|---|
| Memories of a Migrant 1956 | 51 |

# Now

# Between the Wings

Writing the butterfly wings of a poem
should be soft with geometric swirls
of colours that blend with a leaf
or bark of angophora
that stands in the heights
overlooking the sea.
Softness should be embraced
between petals of blue
or the myriad colours
displayed in a garden bed.
The glare of salvia red
or pale green of spring leafing tree
all have their place for the choosing
so flitting from shadow to sun
or slow dripping drift
through the light of day
will create a flow of words
on the page like paint
feather-spread from a brush.

# Memories

memories are such a part of me
when I take one down from the shelf
the smell of the moment
is mine and sometimes aches in its recreation
it will never happen again
but the taste and feel take me out of today
where I lie to watch
two birds in a yellowing tree as the heat
of summer drags me back
to another me in another place
so I see it all again just for a moment
through the same incredulous eyes

but inevitably now
experience shapes the difference

# Maybe

I believe it's important
to try to write
    the unwritable
thoughts which flash
    like flecks of light
on sunlit water
    almost uncatchable
a meeting of lives
in electric collision
    imprinted moments
just dents in the thoughts
    of each intricate self

## Getting Started

Sometimes words rise and fly
like jewelled birds,
orchestrated cries of joy,
but at other times wings fail
and craws clash against the mind,
jumbled letters with discordant sounds
mere shapes perched in tops of trees
unreachable,
to crowd my dreams
with indecipherable vocabulary.
But moving closer to gently stroke
a pair of wings and meet two eyes,
amber bright, I know words
may flow even from this.

# A Lady Bird?

A cockatoo tapped at my window today,
claws gripped the ledge as he peered at me head on one side
    black eye watched, blinked before he turned
to view me with the other, stare with some attention.
I reached for sunflower seeds and he came closer
    grey beak delicately pecking up each seed
        grey tongue curling so he could maybe
imitate my words as he nodded his head.

This was not the same bird I hosed yesterday
hit me on the head with a lemon as I knelt to weed
    showed outrage at the injustice.
Today's bird appeared unaware of my dislike
    made clear his desire for attention.
If I moved quickly he'd fly to nearest branch
wait for a moment of calm then return to feast
    and I thought how wise he was, how clever

so positive patience was rewarded of course
    as he knew it would be and anyway
    maybe it wasn't a 'he' at all
but a 'she' with a female's amazing persistence.

## Some Birds and a Cat

Slicing the sunlight across green of lawn
lorikeets swing over the pergola
to hang upside down from a cage of seed
flash of colour, they give squeaks
and burbles of delight at their find
while neck-thrusting pigeons waddle below
importantly pecking at husks
when my cat   squashed   taut
ears back   green eyes focused slits
begins its
slow motion
stalk
pausing
between
each
stiff
silent
paw pad
on the path
it seems at first the grey birds
on the ground do not see
but the black button eyes of parrots
perceive this may herald moments of terror
so shriek a warning as their wings whirr
to nearby safety of a gum

and the woo-woo-woo of crested pigeons' wings
as they rise now from the ground
let the cat know it's been seen
so the flat stretch of fur releases its tension
and pretending not to be at all put out sits
to lick a paw and wash
nonchalantly elegantly
and deliberately behind its ears.

# The Crested Pigeons at my Window

I wait a while at kitchen window
till rainbow-bright lorikeets
leave with flashes of red and green
screeching their business
to far off trees
then I sneak to feed the pigeons
crests standing stiff and black
wing feathers marked in pinks and blues
all colours clear so daintily precise
they might be made of porcelain
their button brown eyes
watch through window pane
as they perch on wooden sill to wait
being low in the hierarchy
of visitors that come each evening
to graze their fill
peck in bobbing jerks
before light turns soft
warns of approaching dark
so they fly away
with their flute-like sound
to crouch in some unknown place
fluff cuddling through the night.

## Suburban street trees

In summer green
they reach, stretch arms to azure blue
the street below breathes quiet cool
from dappled shadowed sun
till men come to destroy
with whine of saws that drown
the warning shrieks of birds
as brown and broken limbs lie in piles
before they're sucked and chewed
into acceptable bits
so man-made power lines can weave
ugly loops of soiled black wool
to trap possums and unwary birds
that pause in search of food
while black box trees look down
with silent screams of rage.

# Compositions

A rosella's single note
pinprick squeak against roar
of cars and buses down below
it must be across the road
in haven of swaying plane tree
ignoring swish and swoosh
of traffic but darting from branch
to branch hiding in green
of summer growth and I pray
for its safety but know it has no care
for world of men as it flits –
splash of blue and red –
to find its mate
float on air
then sink in some suburban
plot of quiet or in that place where paths
meander through mass of trunks
that lean and twist
to water's edge and mangroves
clump in darkness hiding sky
where fishes gasp in grey of mud
here twilight screech of other birds
is orchestrated symphony of notes
reaching cathedral dome of sky
till the air is filled
with joyful evening songs of praise

# Winter rain

Rain shines on the highway
polishes grey asphalt
streaks of light from lamps
and white ribbons spill
from car headlights
that slide through dark evening light
umbrellas bounce
over huddled dark forms
waiting at nearby crossing
as I watch the parade from high above
like a black crow in the tree that reaches
to brush its bare branches
between my window
and navy winter's night.

# Life in a raindrop

Today I saw a raindrop hang suspended from a leaf
globe of liquid glint in morning light
it slowly stretched towards the earth
fell and disappeared
but I still held the kiss of sun
through the bright diamond
and searched for words to recreate
that moment when translucence
held my life.

# A Roseville Garden

Plants and people have changed
but the maple still stands
drops its round seeds on the path
moss slippery sandstone once
now modern slate-coloured bricks
leading to lopsided
veranda with doors of glass
where the two of them sat
each day for coffee and toast
at ten o'clock sharp
I still hear
their voices gentle and soft
woven through marmalade jam
of morning with shades of green
shaping their world between
newspaper stories that shocked
or caused comment
before cups and plates went inside
when she took up her gloves to kneel
between flowers and weeds
roses, foxgloves, Queen Anne's lace
shaded by deciduous trees
in those long-gone days.

# Night Life

Under the moonlit gaze of night
our garden watches, grows silently
in the dark surrounded by
cacophony of sounds
pond frogs scrape their tunes
in orchestrated joy
small eyes watch for movement
through fluorescent undergrowth
one pounce
a tiny squeal
the rustle of grass
then all is still
while we
continue to dream
through pulsating silvery light

# Drought

Crinkled bark of gum its desiccated skin
reaches from dry corrugations
of parched red earth   branch scrapes against branch
among shiver of leaves   whisperings of desperate thirst
murmurs from gnarled roots below cracked soil
where sheep's skeleton lies   jaw still holding teeth
now agape in recreated agony of final moments shared
    with still and silent heat

a sudden breath of wind   clouds shift and shape
slither across the land drip and spit of relief
as droplets fall in fizz of wet on steaming reach
of every branch and twig   earth sings
each raindrop down gasps to reach for more
but drops recede as clouds reshape in grey-edged mounds
slide beyond horizon's edge and all returns
    to sighs of suffocating dry

## The Nameless

'It may sound dramatic,' she says
'but I wanted to phone before my operation.
I have a brain tumour.
It's most likely benign I'm told – but just in case –'

News headline stares from kitchen table
'Afghanistan deaths increase'.
In front page photographs a general salutes his army
an ambassador shakes hands smiling
Afghani women ululate in newsprint silence

I turn the page
    thinking of my friend.

# In northern winter

Ice hangs stalactites outside my window
and sun's rainbow glints
through pointed frozen fingers
too early yet for warmth to thaw and drip
glass beads onto crisp
thin carpet of white below
where all uncovered
blades of grass stand stiff
encased in crystal coats
every branch of tree is held in silvery vice
while with each whispered January breath
the clash of twig on twig
makes its own winter chime.

# Sea Pictures

White foam crest over blue
swirls to descend in spread
of pounding mist that sprays
in thunderous roar throwing
shell and flotsam
in cascade of silvery light
where froth meets yellow
shore and bubbles rim the edge
at final reach of sea
and footprints dent
then fade from sight
little scratches
of bird claws
dot the sand
among cockles and cowries pale
pink or pearly white reminders
of sunlit glare of day
sitting now in box or tray
abandoned but they still retain
the smell and sounds of
salt rich images of sea.

# Sharks

They glide silently
twist sleek muscular
torpedo shapes as small black eyes
dart to grab passing food
in sharp-toothed open mouths
filter their subterranean world
to gorge on stingrays flapping underwater wings
or minute plankton swirling past in clouds
one of a thousand creatures still alive
eons old before dinosaurs walked
these grey-black monarchs
of innocent grace dance
mythical Scheherazades
in their dark undersea world

I taste the sourness of outrage
when chopsticks ping on porcelain bowls
and spoons scoop soup of fins

# The Innocence of Whales

Huge fountain spurts
silver rods spraying the waves
we can go no closer he says
but his words mean nothing to them
as great puffs and snorts
from circled swirls rise
from ocean depths
dark mounds in blue of sea
one small bright eye winks
so close I could almost stroke the velvet
wet suit slippery of this magic day

    but I can no longer see for tears.

# A visitor to my garden

Purple fruit hang below the twisted vine
I reach to pick succulent grape
gasp and freeze
a pair of eyes look
anxiously down
as I peer up
at the foxlike face the pointed ears
furry body hiding umbrella wings
so we both remain still
surveying each other
I want to stroke him
tell him it's all right
surely a fruit bat is harmless
I move and unblinking he stares
till I withdraw, backwards
slowly as from a king
I have already picked my fill
now it is his turn to eat.

# A Bus Ride

Pink rabbit complete with white tail
gets on the bus after me
followed by two cops young tight-lipped
'Get out of my face,' the rabbit says,
deep-voiced male.
Navy uniforms have followed him
for a while apparently.
'I don't do drugs
never been to jail
I'm not a crim.'
There's dirt on his suit
and his voice is loud.
'Leave a homeless man alone.'
But they don't
ask his name say
he's upsetting passengers.
'Just leave me alone.'
I want to speak
stand up for him
but might make it worse
so wait till cops suddenly leave.
He's alone at last.
'Didn't upset you, did I?' A worried look.
'Not at all. You're just fine,' I say.
His response is
a sunburst gift of a smile.

# The Artists' Camp at Sirius Cove

On the foreshore path the dark earth winds
through clutching undergrowth
and grey-green leaves of gums
with crumpled bark reach out

suddenly a space
of flattened grass where surely Roberts,
Streeton and their friends
will soon return
their laughter and soft voices
murmur beneath screech of birds

beyond this empty space
where boats bob and halyards clink
against their metal spars
the sea still whispers shsh

# Nostalgia

As my journey edges
closer to its end
nostalgia aches
for dappled green of my youth
in limestone hills
where narrow lanes wind
under arch of tree and bush
rivulets from earlier rain
seep down steep banks among boulders
bubble through weed and wild flowers
swirl among birds' cries

contentment must lie with the now
but there are still times
when parrot shrieks
remind me of that other place
stir the tall grasses
to whisper gently in the wind.

## Summer Sunset

Melt as sweat-dripped heat wraps
body to suffocate and itch
pinpricking needles in white glare
toes imprinted on grey tiles
as day's weight drags
to smothering furnace blaze
then glaze of pale blue lifts to tinge of pink
slow spread paint-splashed yellow gold
at last rose turns to red blood fused
with disc of orange sun

# Boonah – an Exhibition by Disability Artists

They're all there;
well-wishers, friends
of the artists though that word
is different for them
they do not conform
live in their own special worlds
are now in the moment
see their creations displayed
splatter and swirl
chaos of light and dark
orange and red
seas purple and blue
sometimes just patterns with names
they've dreamt of or seen in their minds
images snagged in their thoughts
pressed into shapes with finger or brush

I find a bird most likely a duck
Edward Lear design in
turquoise and orange with green beak
which so insistently quacks
I take it home where it hangs on the wall
to welcome those with more prosaic thoughts
so they too can glimpse the joy of that other
sun-flecked world of difference.

# A Breakfast Jam

In the aisle labelled 'spreads'
I reach for raspberry jam
and feel my past in my hand.
Toast in the warm kitchen;
pale winter sun outside;
white starched linen cloth
on table by the window
set with blue plates as scent
of coffee swirls around my grandmother.
Familiar voices
banter and laugh
as we sit watching a red post van,
matchbox size, curl over the green swath
above a farm on the far hill
and thread down looping drive
between patchwork of brown and green fields
to the farmhouse that is my cousin's.
And I recall how when the post van
stopped in the distance and then
began its climb back up the mile-long drive
Grandma put the lid on the jar
and returned it to the larder
though its taste of bee-soaked summer
still lingers round my lips.

# Letting Go

Before you died
there came a time
when I knew
I could no longer go with you
so released my hold
to let you float beyond my grasp
and swirl in soft and misty light
while I stayed at water's edge
not ready then to pass across
that as yet unknown lake.

# Destruction

A bee! A honey bee!
Caught in my kitchen
little wings beat fast
as it circles panic-stricken
I try to guide it to open door
but it decides on another way
I reach for glass and envelope
to catch it on window pane
cover and slide envelope beneath
– hero to the rescue –
it changes course again
must see me glass in hand
at last it flies through open door
into the sunlit garden
where flowers nod and wink.

Headlines read
'Cotton and rice will benefit from floods'
but do not tell
of toxic sprays that kill
and I think sadly still
of my little honey bee.

# Where once I walked

hawthorn hedges form an arch
and green banks slope on either side
towards the narrow lane

crows gossip in skyline trees
above Cotswold homes dug into hills
dry stone walls surround fields
where in between boulders
streams run silver beads
as sway-backed horse munching stolidly
surveys me with lash-framed dark brown eyes
song thrush trills from fallen trunk while
one solitary kingcup thrusts yellow light
from oozing edge of marsh
moss wraps round arms of leaning oaks
which bend to listen
    as I inhale the stillness
        of my beginnings

# A view over the fence

*They plan to demolish the Sirius Building*
*seems wrong to me*
*when I pass it on the bridge*
*stare at its squareness*

'but that's prime real estate
not for the likes of those who live
in public housing – bludgers
and whingers who don't like work'

*it's part of our past*
*modern brutal it may be*
*surely should be preserved*
*for future generations to see*

'not worth saving – ugly as hell
deluxe millionaire jobs should be there
for those who can afford
to pay for harbour view'

*Successful careers*
*and some luck have made us rich*
*so should we not share with others*
*the beauty of this place?*

'I'm not prepared to share
with fucking fools
who cry about unfairness
you get as you give I say'

*a small voice whispers*
   *when did you last give?*

# Reality

The road wound like a ribbon
and below us the green spread out for miles
to the fine line of demarcation
between land and sky
we seemed alone in the universe
until rounding a corner
we found ourselves trapped
behind a long truck full of lambs
tails rammed against the rails
their cries unheeded in the heat
no need to ask where they were going
hanging
throats slit
    blood dripping from hooks

the thought of Sunday roast
slammed against my mind
I could find no excuse

# Remnants

After my mother died I put away her things
so life could resume its pattern
for my stepfather
and memories could be unfolded
only when he wished.
In her wardrobe clothes were alien
with no meaning, not having seen her wear
a dress or coat I found suspended there.
But at the back, protected from the dust,
an old suede jacket still contained
her shape and voice
and when I took it gently down
it held the smell of her
so I recalled those
childhood stories read in bed,
walks down summer-shadowed lanes
and clouds of winter breath
returned her for a moment.

# Transgressions

Once the desert was alive
wells were dug to hold rain
when it came to flood ethe arth
grass seeds held life
men killed only enough to eat with great care
so there was never a shortage of life
on drought-ridden plains
shelters were built
clothes made from beast's skins
words were spoken in soft tongues
land was the source of all life
where souls of the dead
returned to rocks or stars
to watch over those who remained.

    But white man came
believed he knew what was best
would make things as they should be
could not see the country was how it had
always been through thousands of years
such arrogance destroyed the land
killed those living there without thought so
now only dried-out grasses
    shiver sadly in the wind.

## Contrasts

We walk out into winter chill
down the street where people
sit out on footpaths sip coffee
enjoy conversations with friends
as scarves outside shops
smile brightly in July sun
'Barcelona was great.'
'Does your mum approve?'
'It didn't cost much.'
'So what did he say?'

A mattress and unidentified being
rolled in thin blanket in office doorway
blanks out the sun so the winter wind
whips
cold.

# On Flinders Island

Wybalenna, the bird's cry
Flinders Island's haunting tale
where those tortured souls
wept for their birth land
died as they yearned for home.
The chapel stands silent now
watches over those empty graves
as birds wheel and circle above
and black rocks darkly tell
the truth of dreadful lives
while the wind whispers its lament
or sometimes wails against
the sins of those in power
who knew not what they did
or failed to understand
how exiled to that foreign soil
those people died for want of home.

# Northern Territory Shame

How does it feel to have such power?
To be able to fling a boy to the ground?
Is the throat gorged with red rage
in the face of defiance?
Choked by the failure of strength?
Is it hard to say sorry to the smug
look of unrepentant youth?

> Is it only within your personal shell
> that you taste your shame?

# Difference

I stood near an unknown man
thought of the thread
connecting self to self
invisibly spun by no spider
but there just the same.
I couldn't touch nor be sure
it even existed, so shrank back
wanting some secret place
I could maybe join with this other
without knowing him or even his name,
so the space between us
might become nothing at all.

# At this Point in Time

A moment in time
is not a point in space
or a dot a pencil can draw
like a spot on the page
to be rubbed out and vanish
without trace
nor like a being
who leaves a print
an indent on the minds
of others who care or perhaps don't
but have happened to pass
and made contact
to float for a moment
in the same mist of
sharing or misunderstanding
in a second or less
of infinite time

# And Then

# Memories of a Migrant 1956

## 1. The beginning

In dreary queue white breaths plume
through yellow light of lamps'
haze of London damp.
At last a red bus sucks me in
I stand among wet coats
that lean to sway and jerk
past lit-up city shops
towards suburban gloom.
Set down at last I walk
alone along half-lit street.
At every gateway stand
stone lions with Victorian stares.
My footsteps slap the silent dark before
I leave the path and make
my clumsy search
in bag for keys. Inside letter box slit
in front door reveals
crisp blue envelope from overseas
offering escape a month of sea away.
Nerves thrill and clutch
I read the words a hundred times;
'Of course your life is yours,'
my mother, says in tone of voice
that makes me doubt the wisdom of such plans
but ten pounds is all I need.

## 2. At sea

On 'H' deck two-tiered bunks
ride blue surge.
Above thin walls are gaps
whisky fumes spray the dark
night-time words are overheard.
'For God's sake put out that bloody light,'
Irish male voice roars and seasick moans
writhe up from bunk below.

On deck scrubbed boards are wet
from forepeak's rise and fall
through grey-green giants.
Sea froth flicking fingers sting
wild wind coldly tugs and salt smears
lips in fresh chill air.
We climb each curling wave
then plunge back down
through fearful sucking sea.

## 3. Ports of Call

Naples' winter sun slides between
crumbling houses leaning across alleys
women laugh and call in cobbled lanes
our tour bus roars round dizzying curves as
the Italian driver waves his hands and sings.

We slide through Suez
phosphorescent night
daylight sand bites white
in dancing blur of heat.
Long-robed bearded men with obsequious smiles
and missing teeth
hold out bracelets or gaudy rugs
children beg for coins
moth-eaten camels sneer.

Ceylon gives last glimpse of home.

Servants in white tunics
wait on demands from men
who curse in English arrogance.
Brown skins dart through
heat and dust of market wares
expat club requires a limousine
to sit below whirr of ceiling fans.
Vulgarities spew from elegant mouths
before farewells
are made to this 'civilised' place.

On the other side of the world
a bus drives through hot red dust to Perth
where trees sweep long fingers down
to dip in dark of river's edge.
Painted timber houses peer
through grey-green haze of leaves.
Large bellied men in navy singlets
lounge outside red-roofed pubs
flap away flies froth
ringing their lips.

## 4. Arrival

In pink early light we sail through the Heads' great jaws
perched gull-white lighthouse stares
cheers go up. 'Christ! Bloody lovely!' Someone points
to arc of bridge which curves black slash against blue
and bright-coloured houses spill
to water's edge through fountains of green.
The north shore house smells of lavendered old age
but the garden sings of tended plants and trees.
Here grace is said before meals
furniture shines like my host's brown boots.
But I must leave on overnight train for
the New England town
that isn't English at all.

## 5. Workplace

I have a small bedroom
in a boarding school where
constant rain gurgles in downpipes
and girls come in twos and threes
for lessons in good speech.
Here even a magpie's song is as strange
as the pupil's flat voices that
tell of mustering sheep.
I scream in fear when I find a huntsman
but the girls laugh and catch it in bare hands.

On weekends 'jackaroos' come to take
'new talent' to homestead or 'pub'
where women drink schooners of beer
sitting apart from the men to speak
quietly of their own affairs.

I must be approved by the bishop's wife
so at morning tea women in hats
    and beads
look askance but
speak genteel words

    in shadows of drawn blinds
drinking from delicate cups
and nibbling tales of a bygone age.

## 6. Painting Class

Impenetrable twist of trees
recede into canopy of dark
above ferns and grass of undergrowth.
March of green is sliced
by trunks of black and white
with silent cries to living gums.
A fallen trunk is slain man left to die,
reminder of the fight for life
in this unforgiving land.

Not yet familiar with this cutting bright
my paint and brush sees
soft moss greens of English woods
so fails to reproduce the vibrant shades
others splash across the page.

## 7. Meeting by chance

In Brisbane gardens he watches birds
    caged to show their coloured brilliance.
I stand beside him for a while
watch them screech and dance
his eyes brush over me so I am made aware
    and turn to look into ice- blue eyes
    as the kindness of words he speaks
    reach out to draw me in so
    practicalities are cast aside.

## 8. Commitment

I know few at the feast
where windows look out on the Hill's hoist
the keg drips
    and flies
        prance
            on the pink ham.

Men stand in groups while women in hats chat.
'Mrs Green, poor soul, had everything removed.'
    Jewels in their hat pins
        flash when they nod.

This day is not as I expected
not how it would be for my friends far away
    white dress with long train,
    smiles through white veils,
        toasts in champagne

He stands near the tree fern and laughs.
    We are committed for ever
        I know

    I want to believe in our love,
        try to ignore incompatibilities.

## 9. First Home

We rent a place on the edge of town
where timber houses rest on stilts
in regular lines with barren yards
sounds of weekend mowers grind the heat
cars stand with fading paint and peeling vinyl seats
and rusty gates are left to sag.

Red dust blows into rooms
sifting powder onto drapes
bare feet stick to lino floors
and mosquito whines drill the air.
The outside dunny is eerily dark
amid the concert of cicadas' clicks
and honeysuckle fails to hide
the smell of creosote.

## 10. A cleaner's job

Bette, a kindly soul
although at this job for years
is often treated with contempt.
When we're told to clean some doctors' rooms
we find them old with fusty smell
which disinfectant can't remove.
In one of the surgeon's labs
there's something like a woman's womb
lying in an open bin.

We make a fuss
but the doctor says
'You're paid to do the job
so don't complain.'
We feel frustrated rage but
need the work so have to smother it.
When we find huge cane toads
loose among test tubes
we've had enough and quit.

## 11. Shop Girl

In Coles department store
where I work for a while
an eighteen-year-old is counting socks.
'I'm not pregnant, the doctor says
but me teeth have got to go.
Me hubby, Wayne, says he don't mind.
he'll love me just the same,
I can cover me mouth with me hand
like this, I said.
It's scary, but,' she adds.
'Poor kid,' an older woman with crimped hair
mutters to her friend over lunch.
'So young and just a bride.
They'll certainly find out
what life is all about and what it means
to say "For better or for worse."
Not that loss of teeth will alter sex.'

She mouths the last unmentionable word
and drinks her lukewarm tea
to help swallow the powdered Bex
she always takes straight after lunch.
'The way *she* talks about it makes me think
the young have got no pride…or shame.
Disgusting really. I've always felt
*that* is a thing men say *they* need, not us.
*We* think of higher things, my mother said
and she was right, I'm sure, but girls like that
seem keen. Can't think why!' She sniffs
to emphasise her loathing for the word
and what it means then
gathers up her sandwich box
to check the takings in the till.

## 12. Memories

Nostalgia aches in Christmas heat
when whirs of fans never cease
harsh-voiced men tell tales
lounging to drink cold beer
children search plum puddings
for a sixpenny piece.

*But I see mistletoe berries of white;*
*crunch of steps*
*in crispy cold*
*scarves and gloves*
*fire flames' dance with*
*ticking clock in the living room.*

August winds lift linoleum floor
kerosene heater always burns while
in wintery yard yellow fluff balls
fly from arms of wild wattle tree
and cracked-lipped children smell
of Vicks rubbed nightly into chests.

*But I see a pebbly beach*
*deckchair in gentler sun*
*near sea-swilled pools*
*in cool grey rocks*
*as seaweed lifts and falls*
*to hush with the tides.*

## 13. The Brisbane River

Brown snake river writhes
through murky mangrove swamps
fish breeding among the roots.
Set high to catch the breeze, houses
flash through tropical growth where
all is still in the stifling air
sliced by cicadas and birds' cries.
Further down in river's lazy flow
factory chimneys stand on either side
where iron sheds spill crates
of sludge with vile smell
into dirty waters' gravied gloom.

Once pelicans were here but now
only gulls bob on coffee froth of river's flow
while brooding at dark water's edge,
black-eyed bats hang rags from trees
rising at dusk in circled shrieks
to suck noisily at pungent fruit.

## 14. Lessons

Children screech and flap like birds
at a convent school where I teach
they run in lace-up shoes
slap, crack, on asphalt yards
corridors smell of polish and stale apples.
Painted stick figures hang below
pictures of present-day Christs
clean-shaven golden-haired dressed
in white flowing robes

Framed prints of hearts bleed into minds
as nuns with soft voices, but firm like the sticks
of dusters they keep in their desks for use
on small hands, dispense lessons and love.
After times tables are sung Hail Marys are said
for the priest who comes once a week
to the red-brick building and asks
about 'Mummy's new baby' or 'Daddy's new job'.
The children's eyes shine as he laughs and jokes

but I know I don't belong.

## 15. Bus Ride

The road shimmers in early sun
promise of greater heat to come.
Trees at the bus stop give umbrella shade
as a group of women climb the hill.
Pageant of gloves, beads and hats
they stand to fan themselves and pat
their upper lips with lace-edged handkerchiefs.
'So I said to him, I'm not real pleased –
course Len and Marg give in to him
say I don't understand the way it is
today but should accept things change –
still, I think he oughta spend more time
on learning maths, but he just says,
I won't need that in the army, Gran.
That's what you think,' I said.
'All he thinks about is sport an' that.
Well, 'course I know outdoors is good
but when he said he'll prob'ly fail
because of maths, I said,
I'm not real pleased
the army won't have you,' I said, 'then what?'
The jolting bus arrives as words still
bounce from under hats
and pleated skirts perch
on sweat-hot vinyl-covered seats
as we wind slowly into town
stopping only to receive more hats
or men in shorts, long socks
and rolled-up sleeves.

The women rise at journey's end.
'Yes, linen creases terrible, I say.'
Till drowned by other city sounds
voices melt in Brisbane summer's day.

## 16. Queensland Radio Days

As the music fades the producer
in his smoke-filled room
perfunctorily nods
so the program may begin.
With both feet firmly planted
hands steady so the script won't shake
the mic devours my childlike voice.
'Where are we going today, Uncle Jim?'
We wander through imaginary bush
introducing nature's gems
as each week this science tale
is beamed to every primary school.
Uncle Jim is a well-known voice
experienced in radio ways
and in a second's pause one day
gently lifts his old tweed coat
a pair of eyes in brown grey fur
wink and blink in the light.
'I see, Uncle Jim, it's not fungus at all…'
My eyes are on the final page
the producer is happily unaware
as the possum nibbles a piece of fruit.
'Uncle Jim' teasingly grins
at my attempts to keep to script.

## 17. Maroochydore Holliday

The cream verandaed house
stands high on timber stumps.
Beyond green grass strip the river writhes
through mangrove swamps
waterbirds spill their mournful calls
gulls flash white with wheel and screech.
From where dark river meets wide sea
the village curves round sandy beach
iron roofs creak in summer heat
water tanks snug against house walls
frangipanis drip pink petals to lie
beneath tall rustling palms
whose dead fronds drape round lumpy trunks
while rich fruit bulge in leaf-thick mango trees.
On hot white sands waves curl and fall
white froth of foam as children search for pipis
at rippled water's edge. Sun hats, floppy brimmed,
bounce and bob across the sand
while mothers watch like owls.
Houses frown against bright glare
of sun and at each shop door hang
strings of beads which I must part to leave
with sound of bottles clink to call my child
who licks from salt-dried fingers
sugared juice of water ice.
Squealing children run barefoot down dirt paths
piercing summer's lazy ways.

Irrelevant time merges day with day
over my bed at night the net
hangs guard against mosquito's wine
while in moon's soft glow of light
sand-streaked floorboards shine.

## 18. Shopping From Home

Everything comes to the door.
The ice man, the baker, the dunny man too
runs down the path
with slop and spill.
The fisho comes with eager flies,
and cake-o man, moustache like a brush,
whose open-sided truck
reveals delights so child's eyes shine.
'One of those and one of those.
Oh, that one too.' Rustle of notes
clink of change as lips ooze cream
and chocolates smeared down shorts
stained from red mud games.

The library comes in a bus
few climb inside
to choose a Christie or Mills and Boon.
Twice a week the Chilean man
face a wrinkled prune
claims to be over eighty-six
honks his horn to bring housewives.
Fingers curled like a claw
pull beans from a sack while the women chat

    standing
        waiting
          string bags
            dangling
'Yes, little lady?'
In truck's cool shade
gossip mingles with beans.

## 19. Cultural Changes

On Saturday nights young ones go
in Holden cars sitting in rows
to stare at sky-surrounded screen
where Marilyn wiggles.
White plug-in posts
carry speakers so her husky voice
seems to belong
to the girl in the next door car who sighs
as rough hands fondle soft breasts.

After closing time
crowds stand outside shops
to stare inside
at a black and white TV screen
advertisements for Ford pills
men in dinner jackets smile
eager questioning eyes learn
of other ways to live.

Eating out meant
T-bone steak and chips
at Formica tables roughly wiped
with rags smelling of onion rings
but in the sixties pasta appears
wound in long yellow strings
round forks while candles glow
from empty green bottles of wine.

Languorous summer days
unfurl so I limply drag
along stifling city streets
but now among floral prints,
women in black
wave their hands as they speak
in foreign language that sings.

## 20. A part of the place at last

On holiday in Cairns the heat
sits on our heads like bricks
cane toads squat on paths to spit
at boys who use them as cricket balls.
Evening bats wing, flapping black cloaks
as their eerie cries
tear at the night's dark blue
while cockroaches race across floors
or wave feelers as they pause
to choose their next place to hide.
By day it's greener than green outside.

We walk on the beach
where no one has been,
it appears, for a week
and our footprints leave
marks in hot white sand
which even the tide might not reach.
Beside Mossman Gorge we throw down
our clothes and swim
in the velvety cool
among swirling fish
as soft sand glints
between sunburnt toes
while above rainforest vines
weave to the light
in the peace of this place,
millennia old.

I breathe in the scene
as a bird threads its song through the trees.

www.ingramcontent.com/pod-product-compliance
Lightning Source LLC
Chambersburg PA
CBHW062156100526
44589CB00014B/1852